This book belongs to:

Mission 1:

Trace the letters and the numbers

Aa

A is for apple

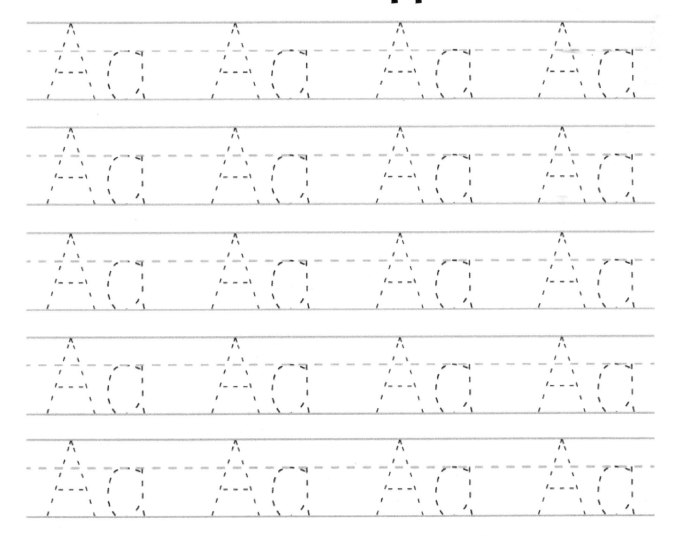

Bb

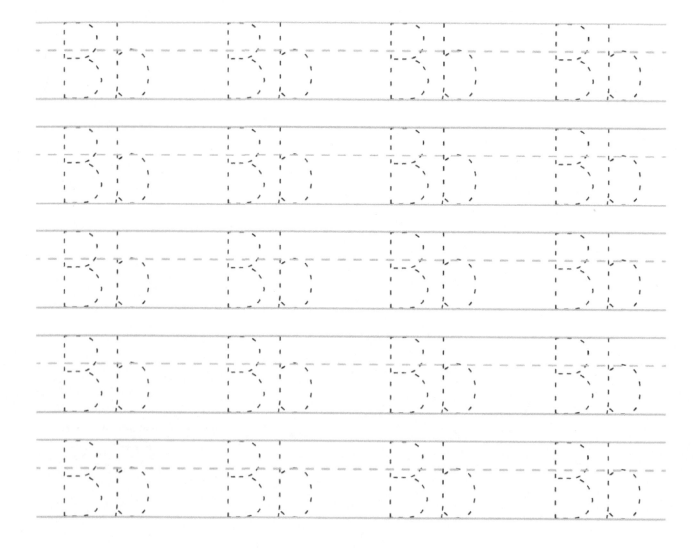

B is for bear

Bb Bb Bb Bb

Bb Bb Bb Bb

Bb Bb Bb Bb

Bb Bb Bb Bb

Bb Bb Bb Bb

Cc

C is for car

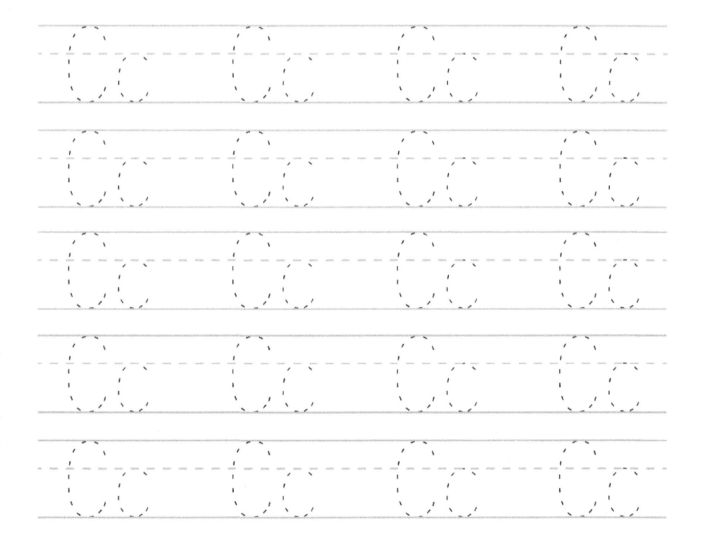

Dd

D is for dog

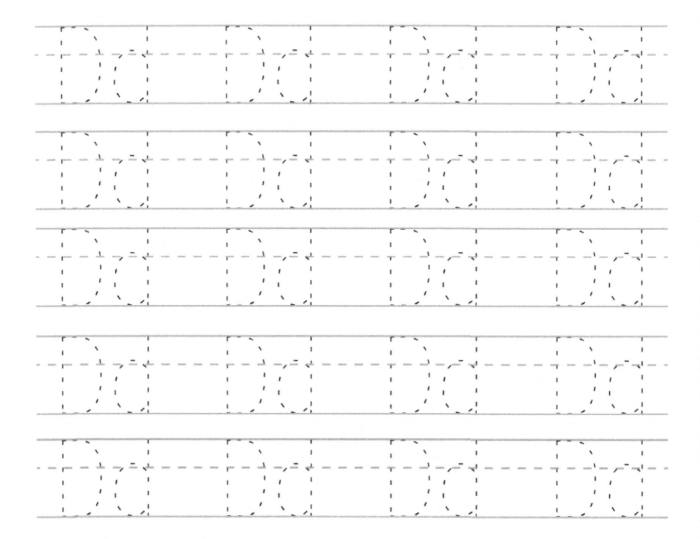

E e

E is for elephant

Ee Ee Ee Ee Ee

Ee Ee Ee Ee Ee

Ee Ee Ee Ee Ee

Ee Ee Ee Ee Ee

Ee Ee Ee Ee Ee

Ff

F is for frog

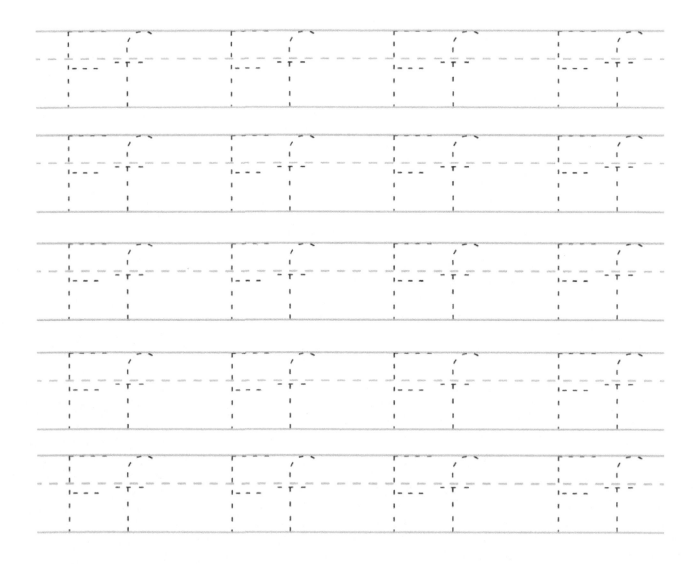

Gg

G is for goat

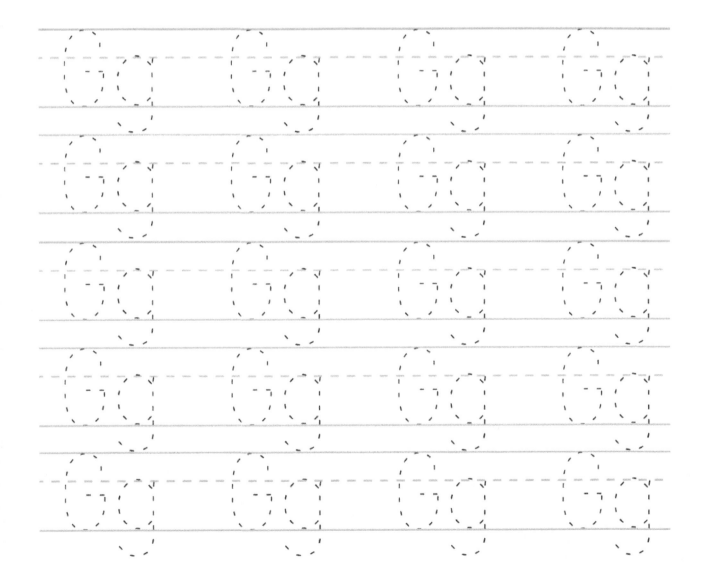

Hh

H is for hippo

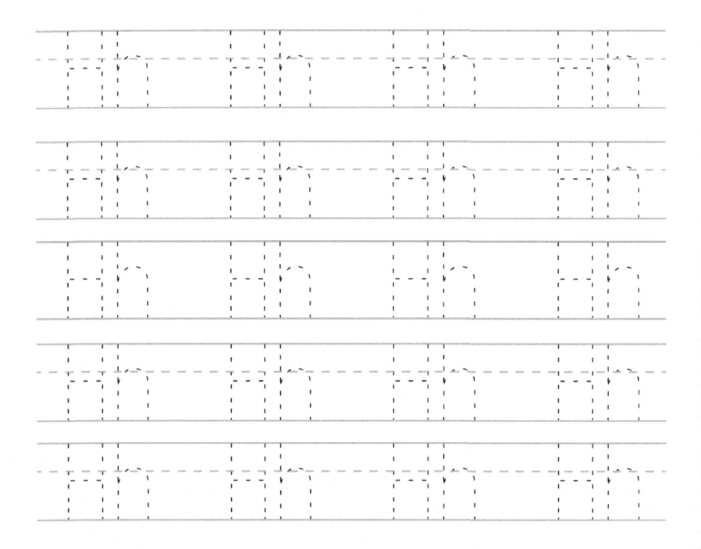

I is for igloo

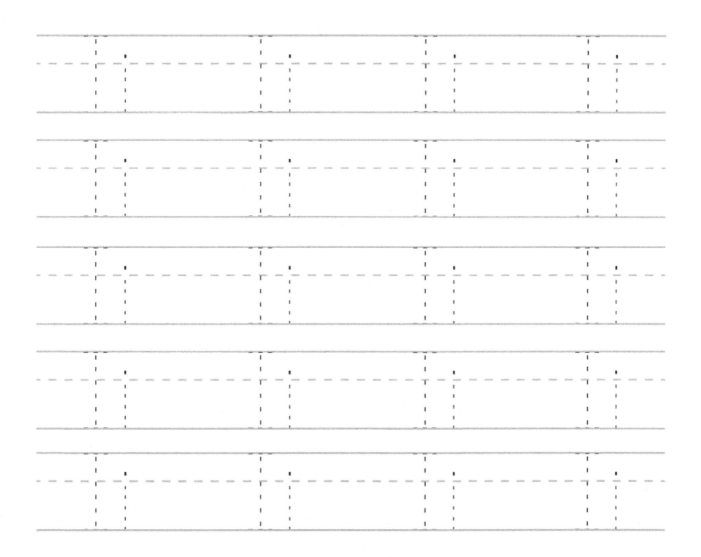

Jj

J is for jaguar

Kk

K is for key

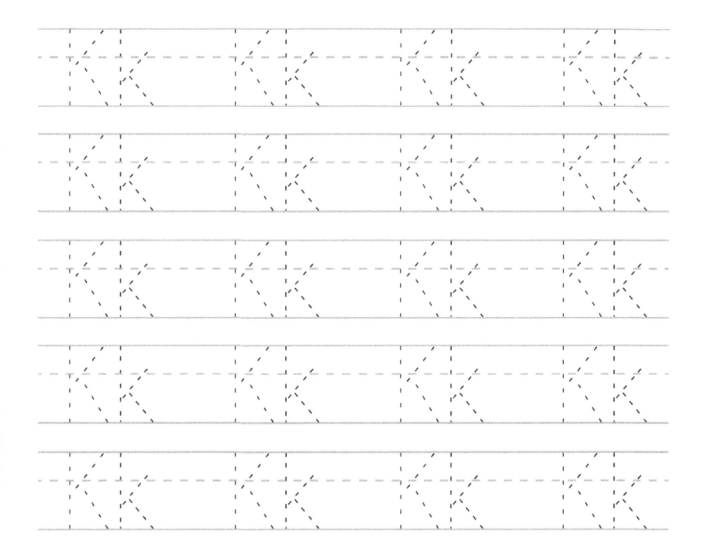

Ll

L is for lion

Mm

M is for monkey

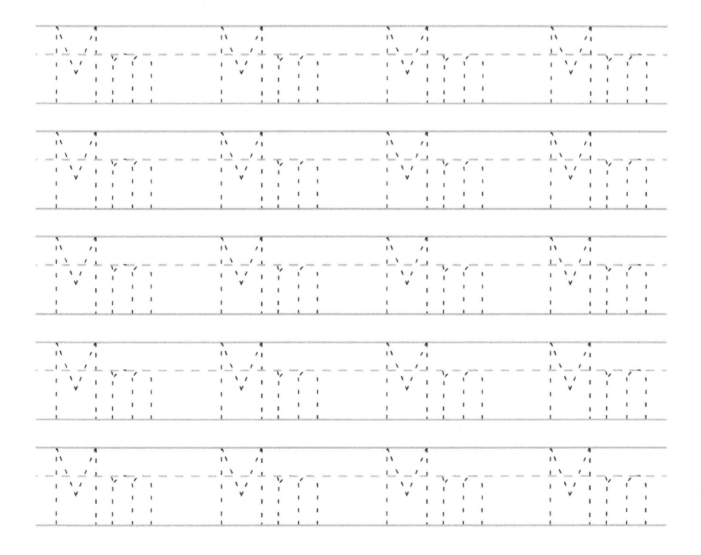

Nn

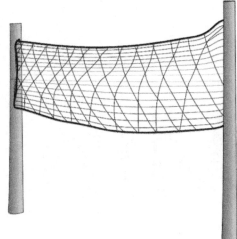

N is for net

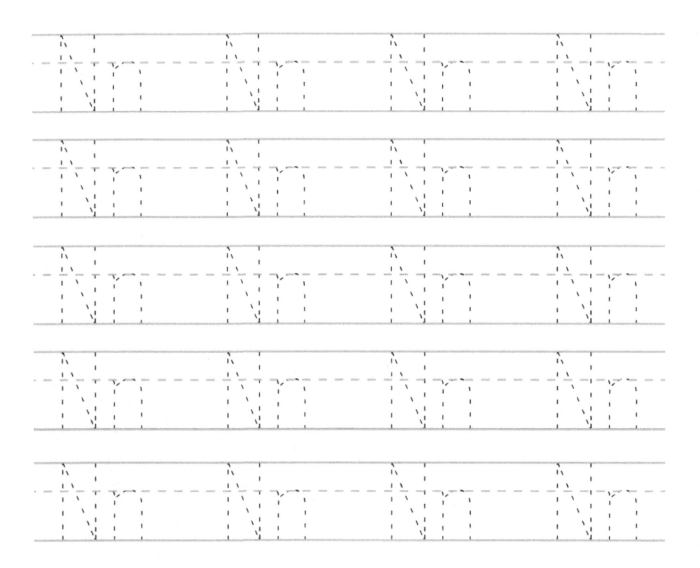

Oo

O is for octopus

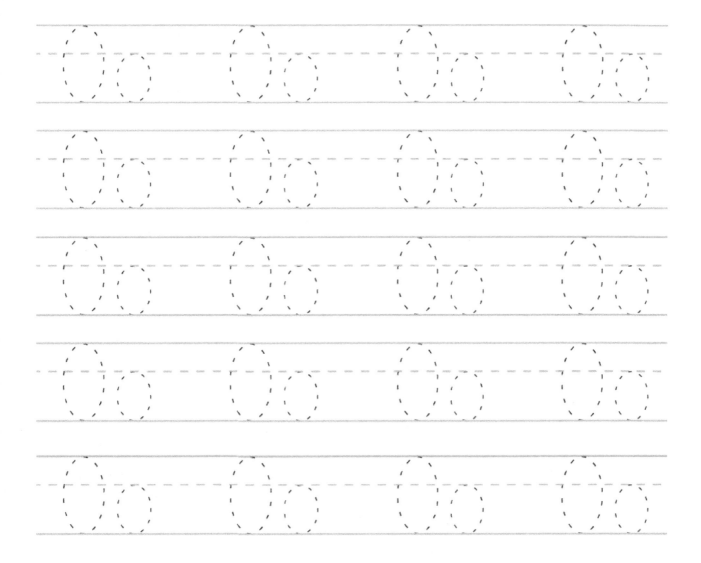

P p

P is for parrot

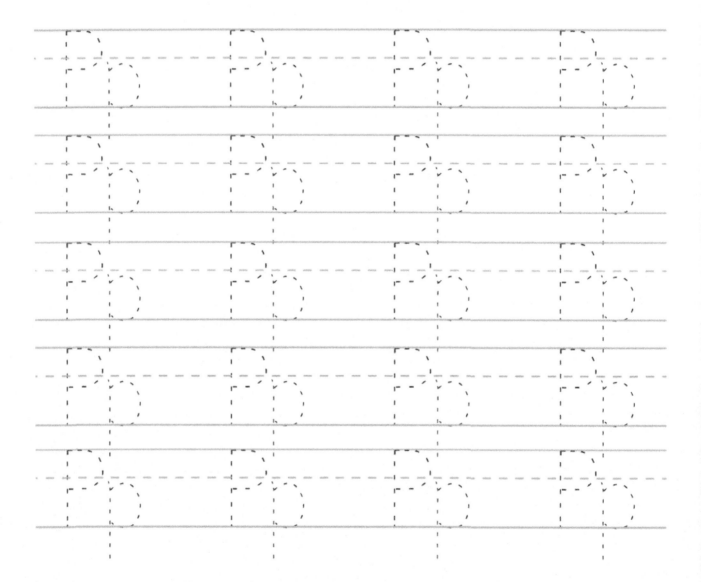

Qq

Q is for quail

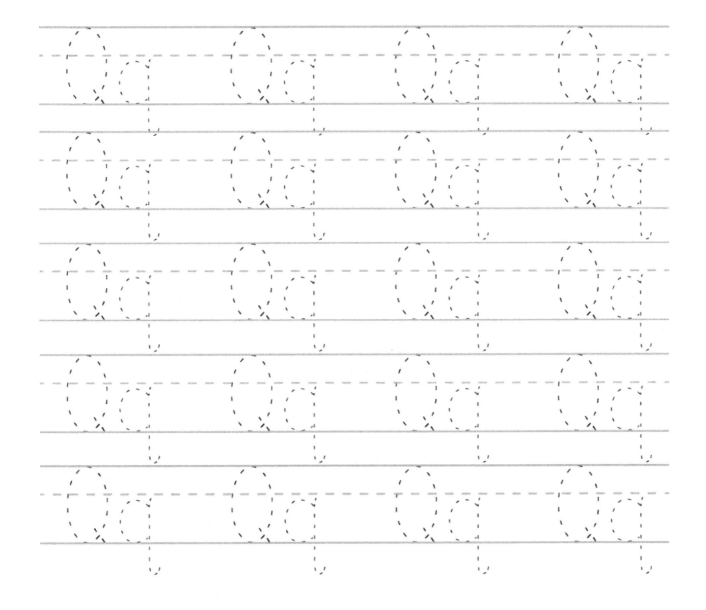

Rr

R is for rabbit

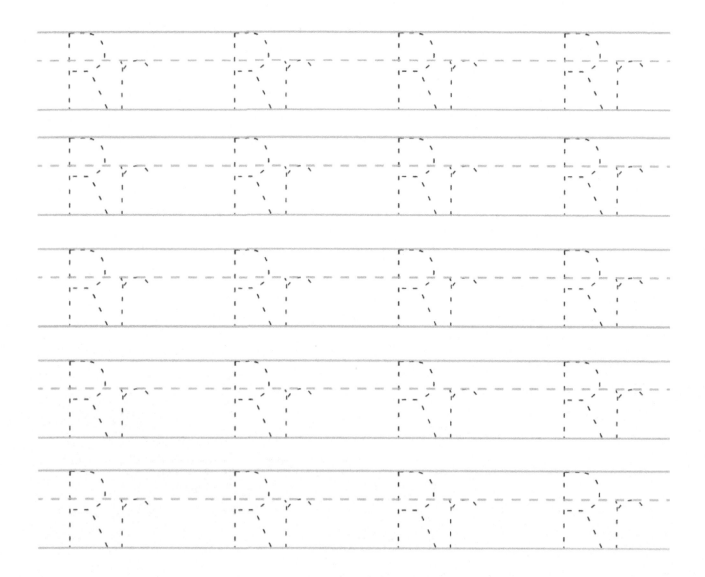

Ss

S is for snail

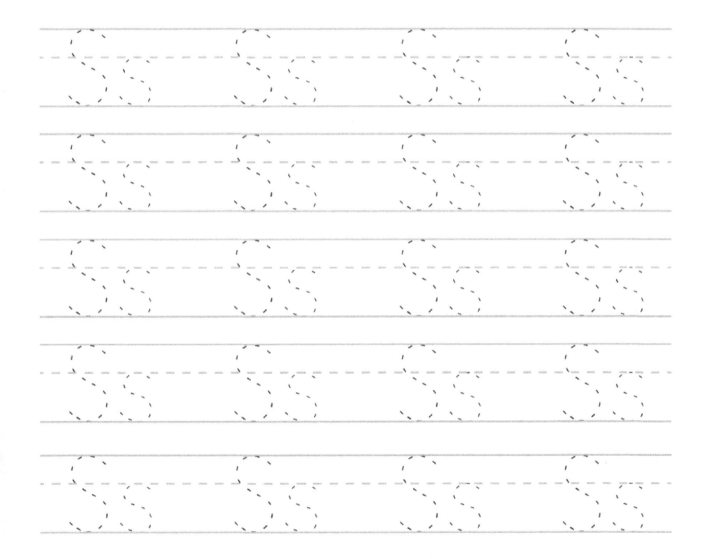

Tt

T is for turtle

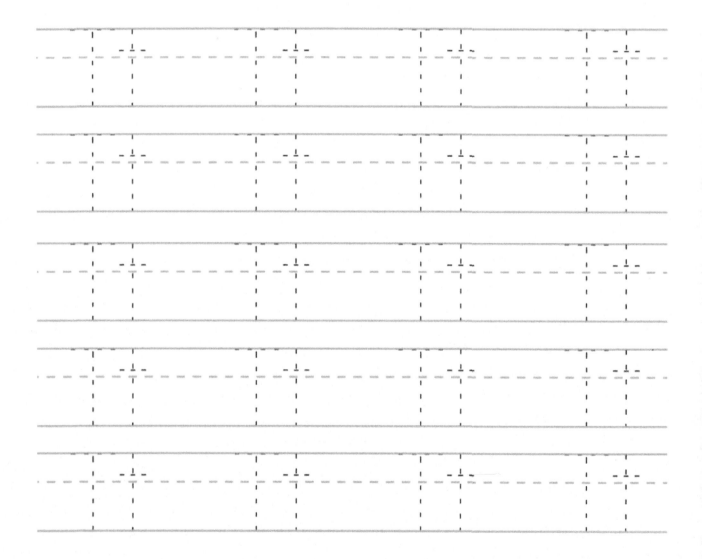

Uu

U is for umbrella

Vv

V is for violin

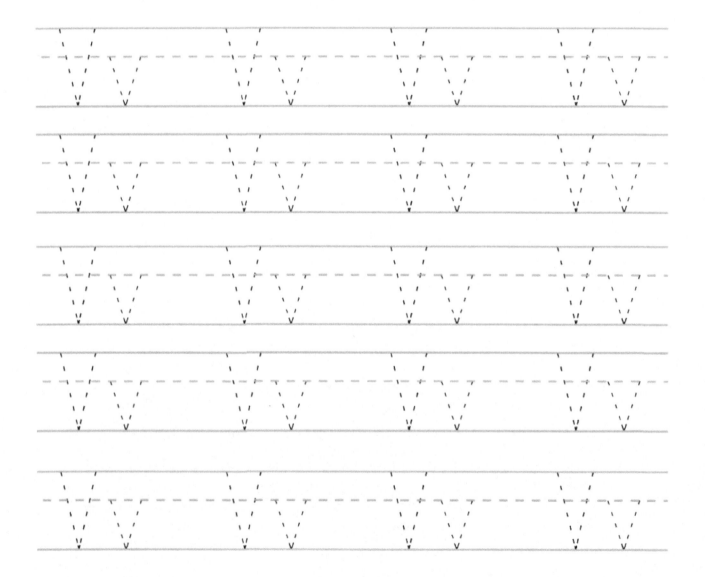

Ww

W is for whale

 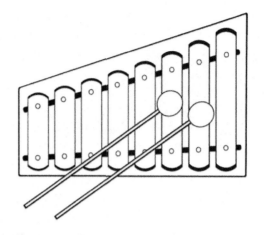

X is for xylophone

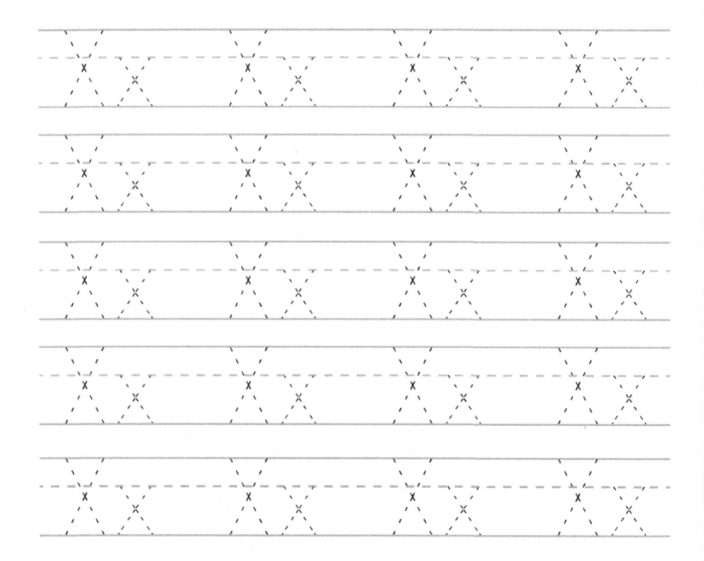

Yy

Y is for yak

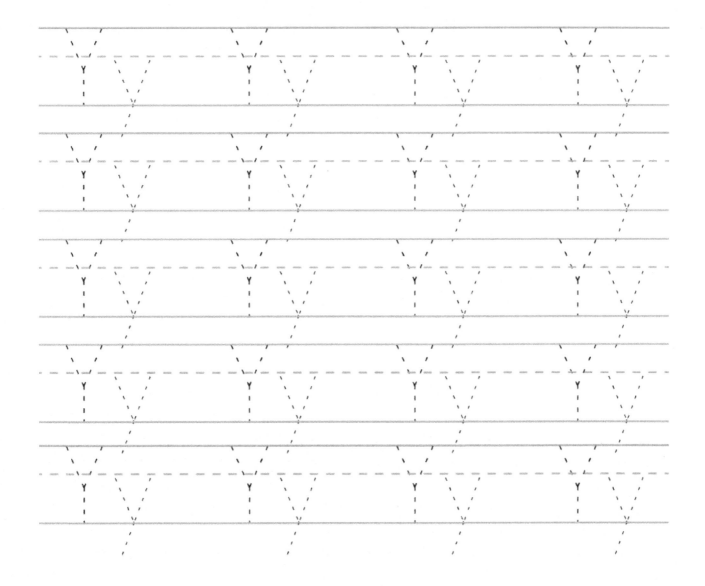

Zz

Z is for zebra

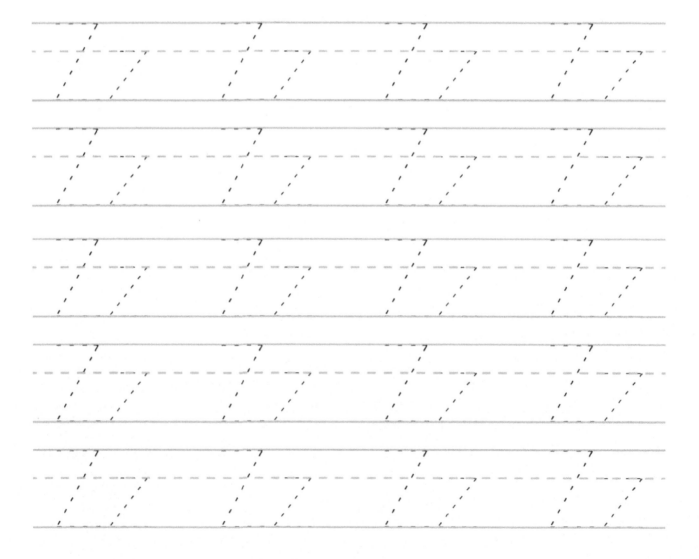

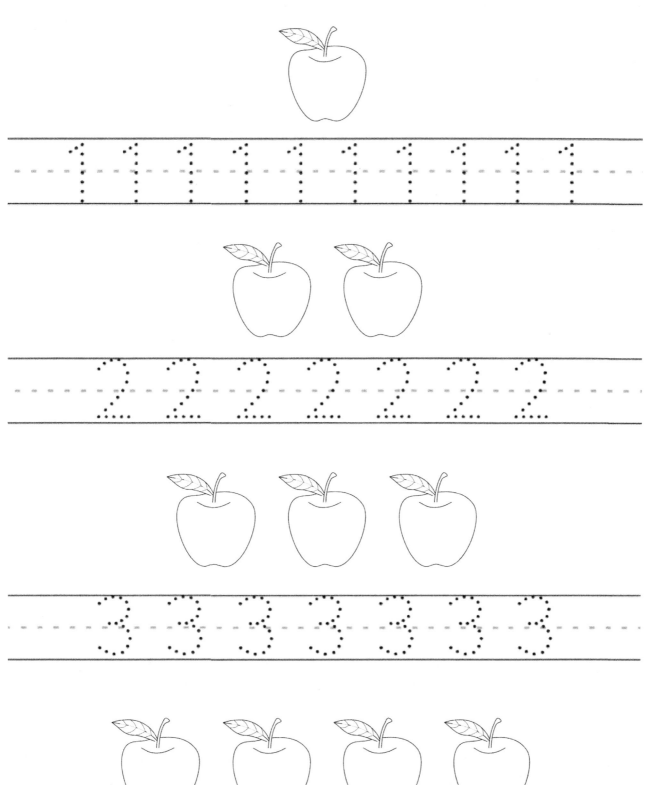

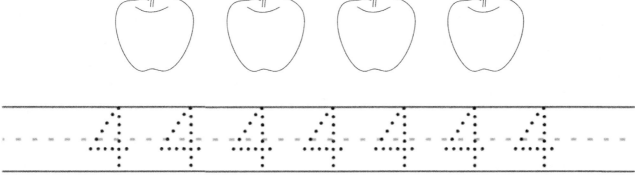

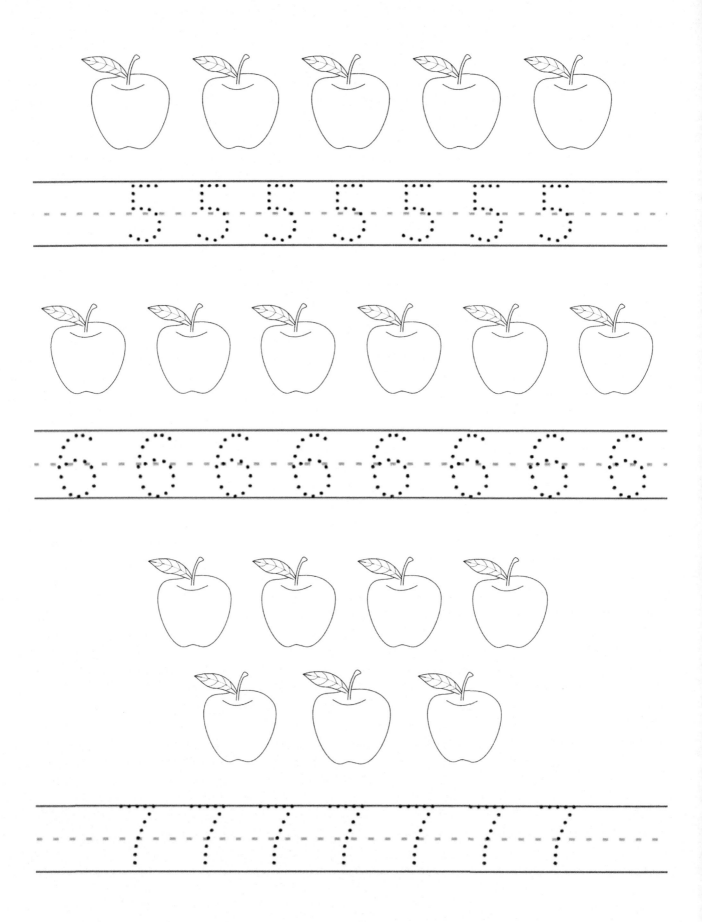

Mission 2:

Colour and create drawings and trace the words

Colour the drawings that begin with the letter A, and fill in the blanks
with drawings of other words that start with A.

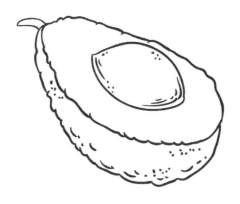

avocado

Colour the drawing and trace the word

Colour the drawings that begin with the letter B, and fill in the blanks with drawings of other words that start with B.

bear

Colour the drawing and trace the word

Colour the drawings that begin with the letter C, and fill in the blanks with drawings of other words that start with C.

COW

Colour the drawing and trace the word

Colour the drawings that begin with the letter D, and fill in the blanks with drawings of other words that start with D.

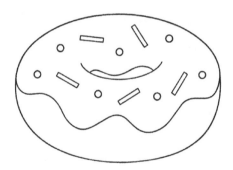

donut

Colour the drawing and trace the word

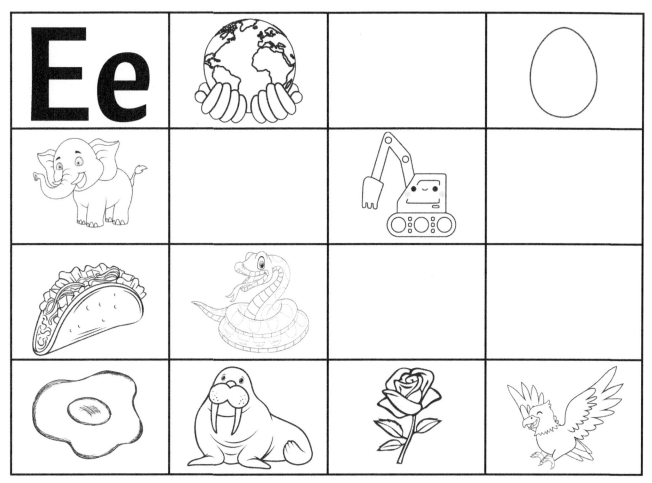

Colour the drawings that begin with the letter E, and fill in the blanks with drawings of other words that start with E.

elephant

Colour the drawing and trace the word

Colour the drawings that begin with the letter F, and fill in the blanks with drawings of other words that start with F.

fish

Colour the drawing and trace the word

Colour the drawings that begin with the letter G, and fill in the blanks
with drawings of other words that start with G.

grapes

Colour the drawing and trace the word

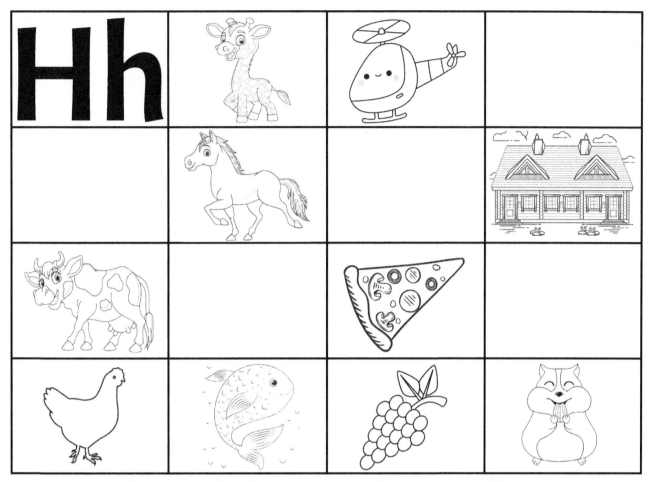

Colour the drawings that begin with the letter H, and fill in the blanks with drawings of other words that start with H.

hamster

Colour the drawing and trace the word

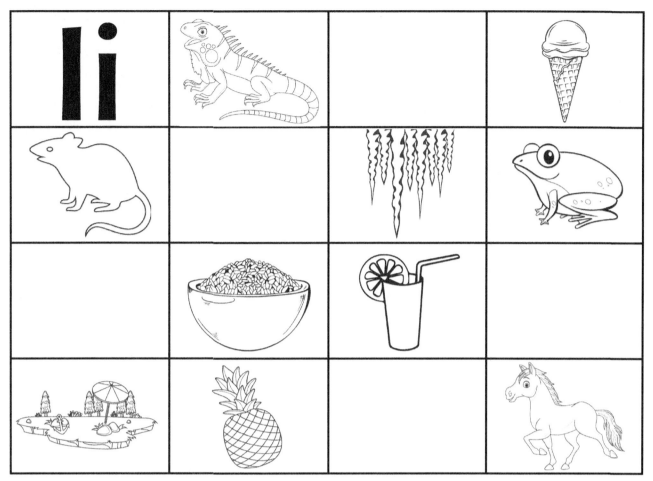

Colour the drawings that begin with the letter I, and fill in the blanks with drawings of other words that start with I.

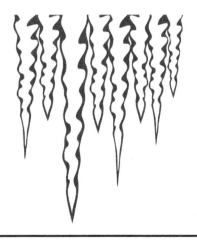

icicles

Colour the drawing and trace the word

Colour the drawings that begin with the letter J, and fill in the blanks with drawings of other words that start with J.

jaguar

Colour the drawing and trace the word

Colour the drawings that begin with the letter K, and fill in the blanks with drawings of other words that start with K.

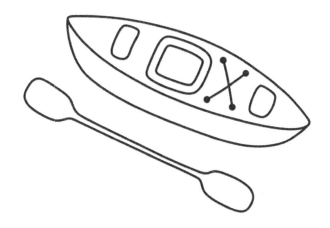

kayak

Colour the drawing and trace the word

Colour the drawings that begin with the letter L, and fill in the blanks with drawings of other words that start with L.

leaf

Colour the drawing and trace the word

Colour the drawings that begin with the letter M, and fill in the blanks with drawings of other words that start with M.

mango

Colour the drawing and trace the word

Colour the drawings that begin with the letter N, and fill in the blanks with drawings of other words that start with N.

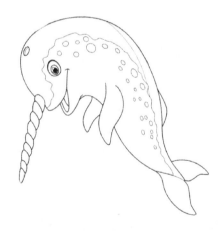

narwhal

Colour the drawing and trace the word

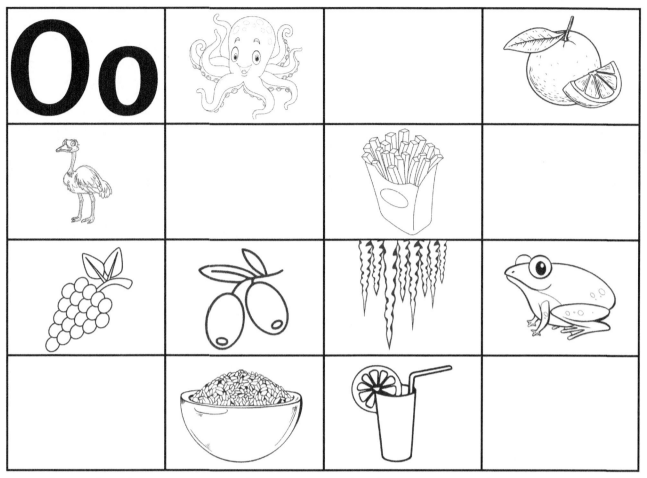

Colour the drawings that begin with the letter O, and fill in the blanks with drawings of other words that start with O.

ostrich

Colour the drawing and trace the word

Colour the drawings that begin with the letter P, and fill in the blanks with drawings of other words that start with P.

pizza

Colour the drawing and trace the word

Colour the drawings that begin with the letter Q, and fill in the blanks
with drawings of other words that start with Q.

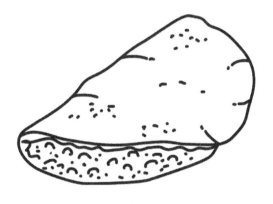

quesadilla

Colour the drawing and trace the word

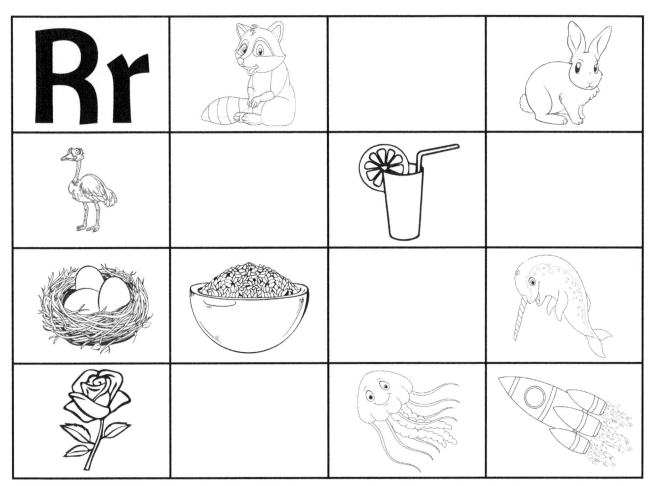

Colour the drawings that begin with the letter R, and fill in the blanks with drawings of other words that start with R.

rice

Colour the drawing and trace the word

Colour the drawings that begin with the letter S, and fill in the blanks with drawings of other words that start with S.

sandwich

Colour the drawing and trace the word

Colour the drawings that begin with the letter T, and fill in the blanks with drawings of other words that start with T.

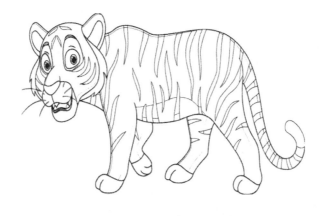

tiger

Colour the drawing and trace the word

Colour the drawings that begin with the letter U, and fill in the blanks
with drawings of other words that start with U.

ukulele

Colour the drawing and trace the word

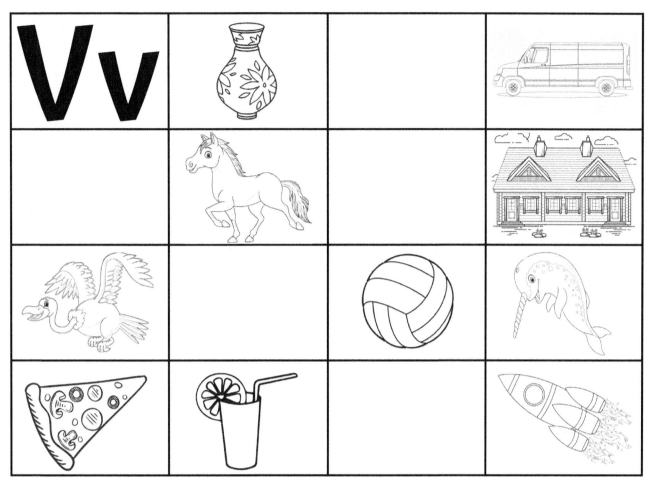

Colour the drawings that begin with the letter V, and fill in the blanks with drawings of other words that start with V.

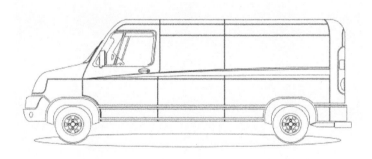

van

Colour the drawing and trace the word

Colour the drawings that begin with the letter W, and fill in the blanks
with drawings of other words that start with W.

watermelon

Colour the drawing and trace the word

Colour the drawings that begin with the letter X, and fill in the blanks with drawings of other words that start with X.

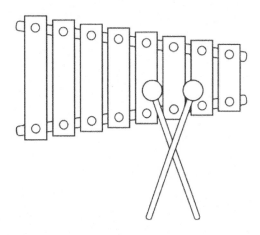

xylophone

Colour the drawing and trace the word

Colour the drawings that begin with the letter Y, and fill in the blanks with drawings of other words that start with Y.

yak

Colour the drawing and trace the word

Colour the drawings that begin with the letter Z, and fill in the blanks
with drawings of other words that start with Z.

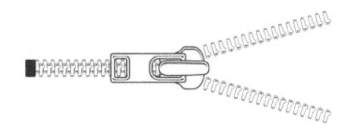

zipper

Colour the drawing and trace the word

Congratulations!
2 missions done
2 more to go!

Mission 3:

Find the letters

Find the letters.

is for apple

Find the letters.

_____
B
_____

is for bear

B   C   F   B

U   B
G   K
R

O   Z   B   X

Find the letters.

_____
(C)
‾‾‾‾‾‾‾‾‾‾‾‾‾‾‾

is for car

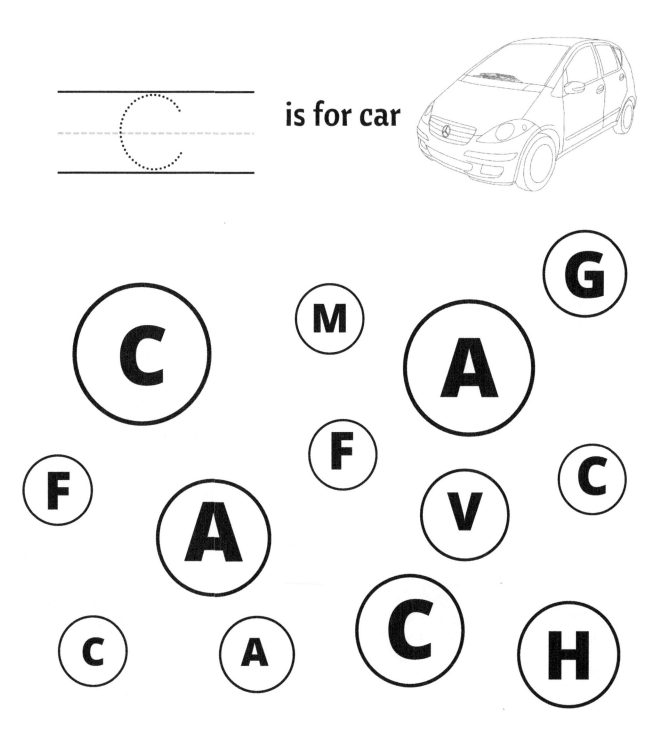

C M G A

F F V C

A C

C A H

Find the letters.

is for dog

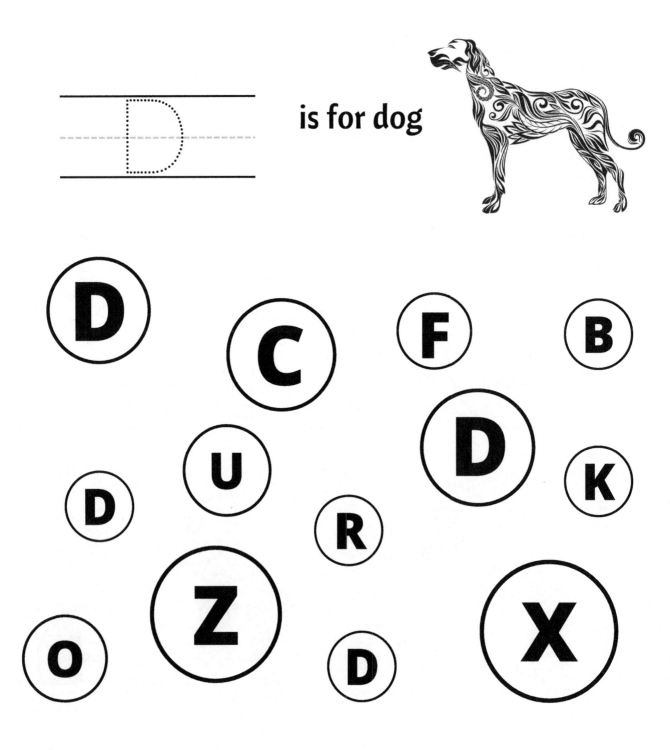

Find the letters.

E is for elephant

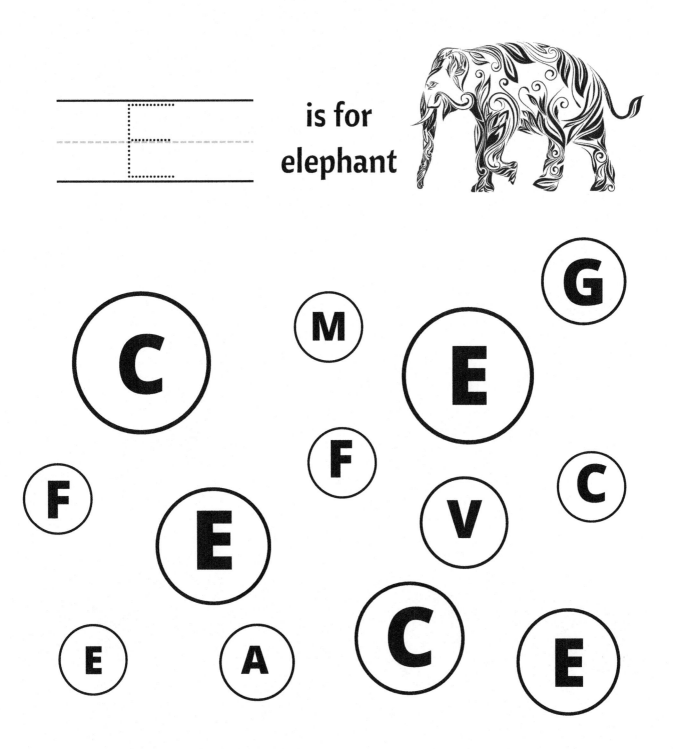

Find the letters.

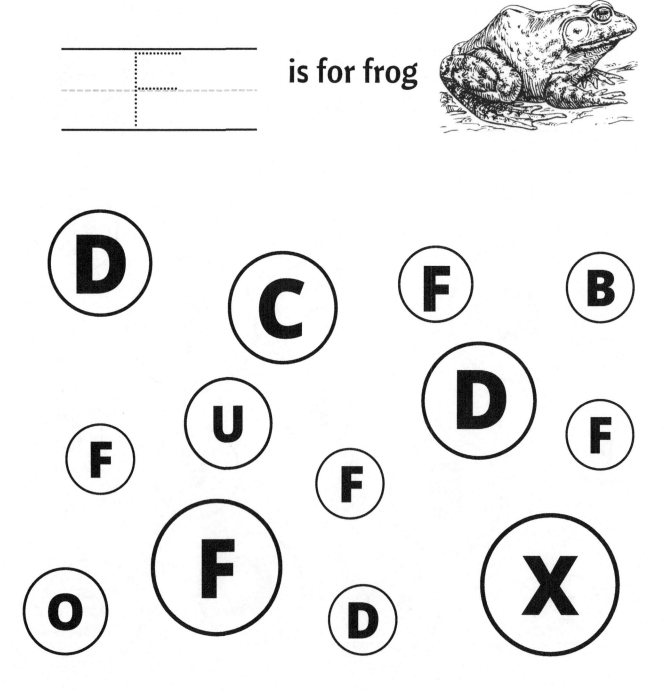

____F____ is for frog

Find the letters.

___G___   is for goat

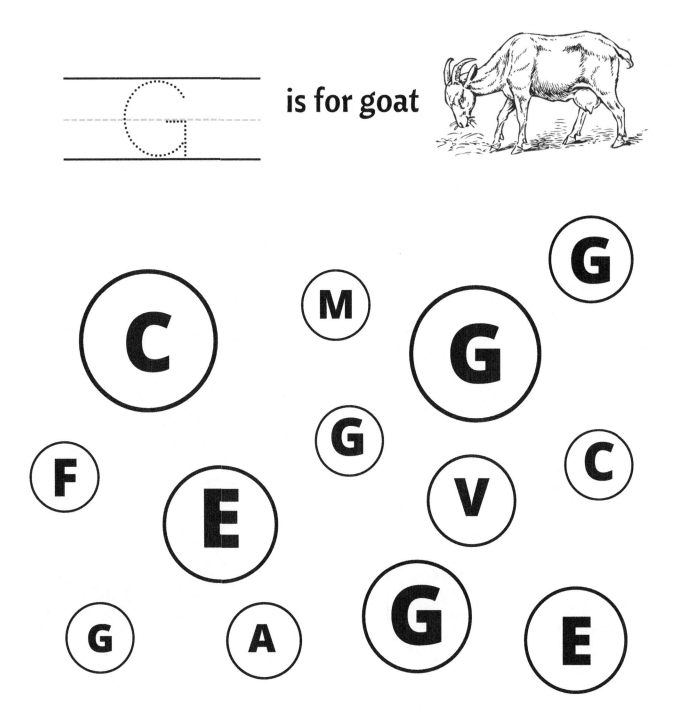

Find the letters.

H is for hippo

Find the letters.

_____ is for igloo

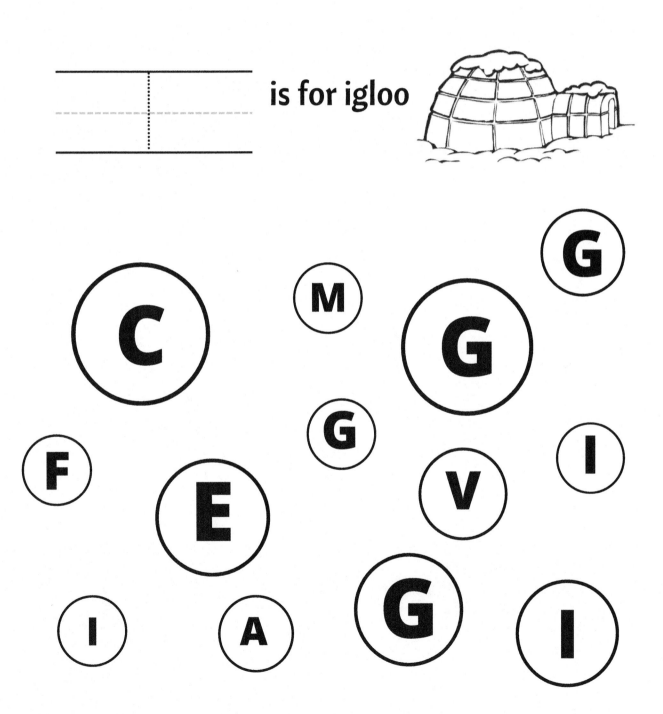

Find the letters.

_____ J _____ is for jaguar

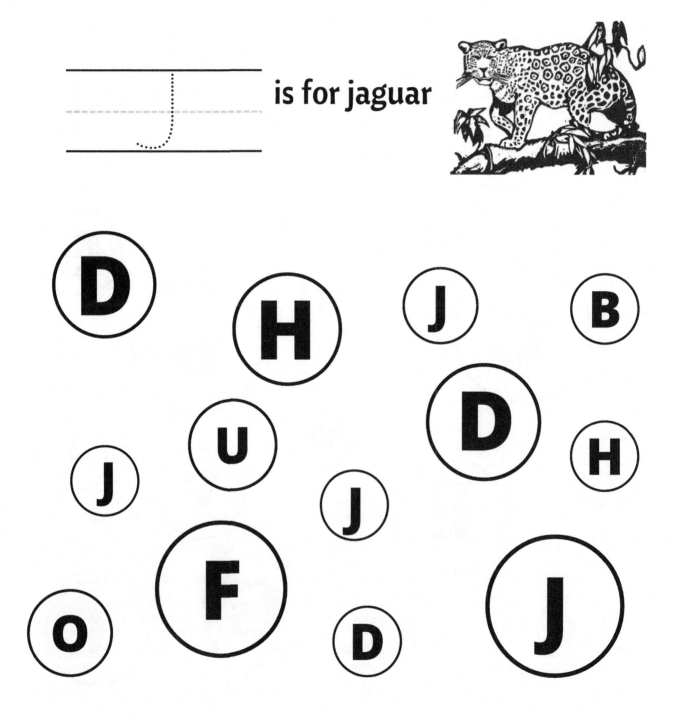

Find the letters.

K   is for key

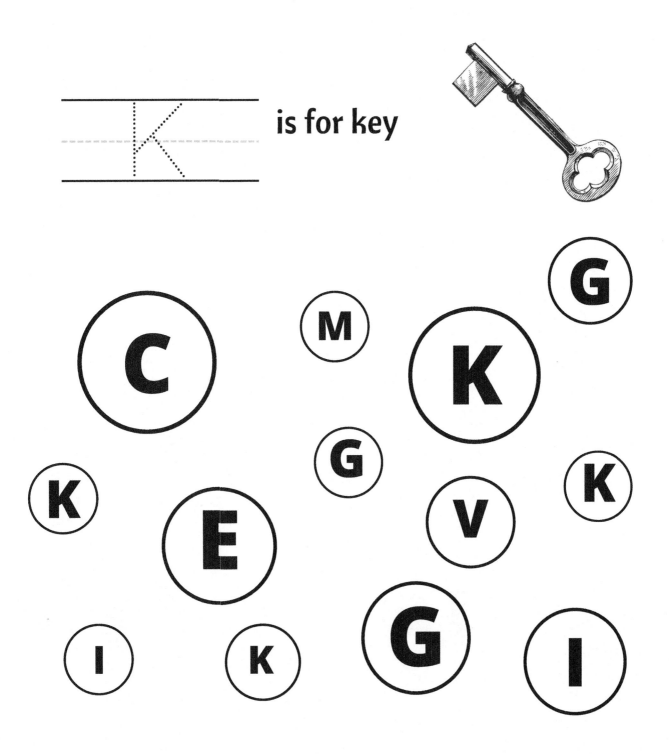

Find the letters.

is for lion

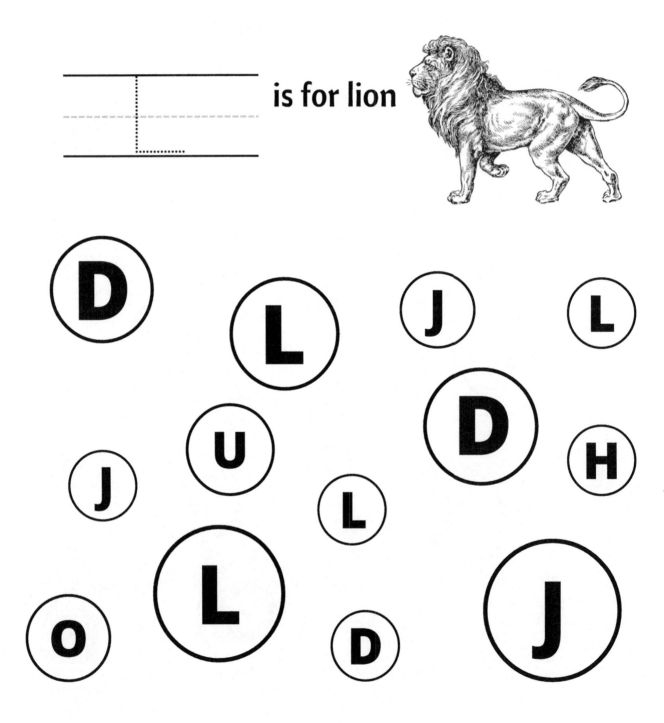

Find the letters.

M ____ is for monkey

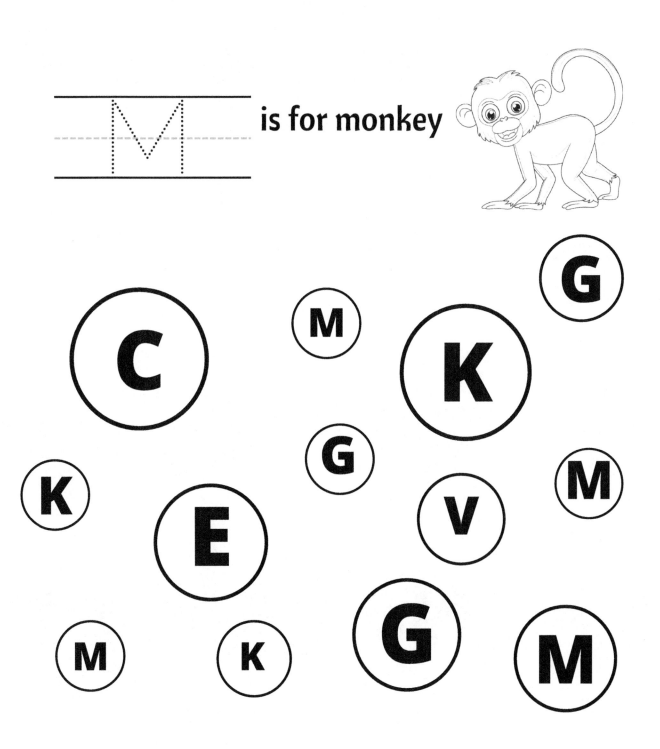

Find the letters.

N is for net

Find the letters.

_____ is for octopus

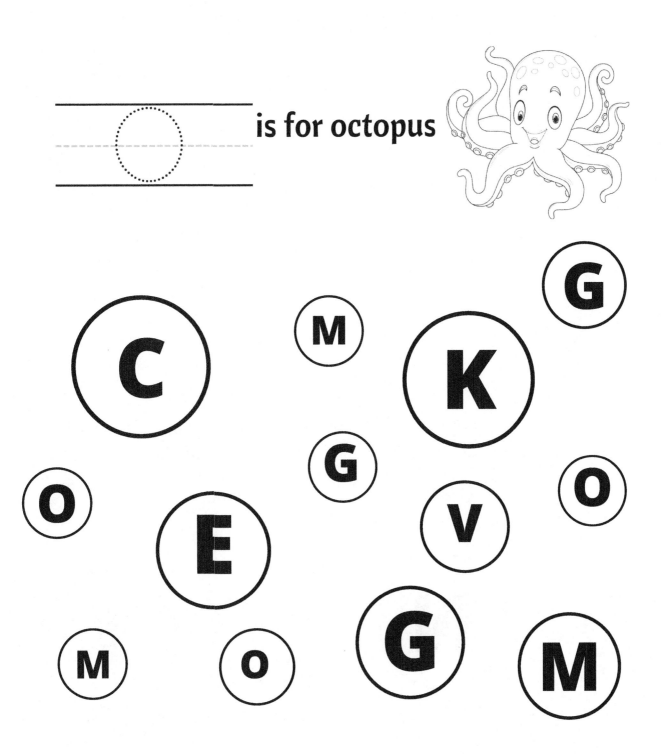

Find the letters.

P

is for parrot

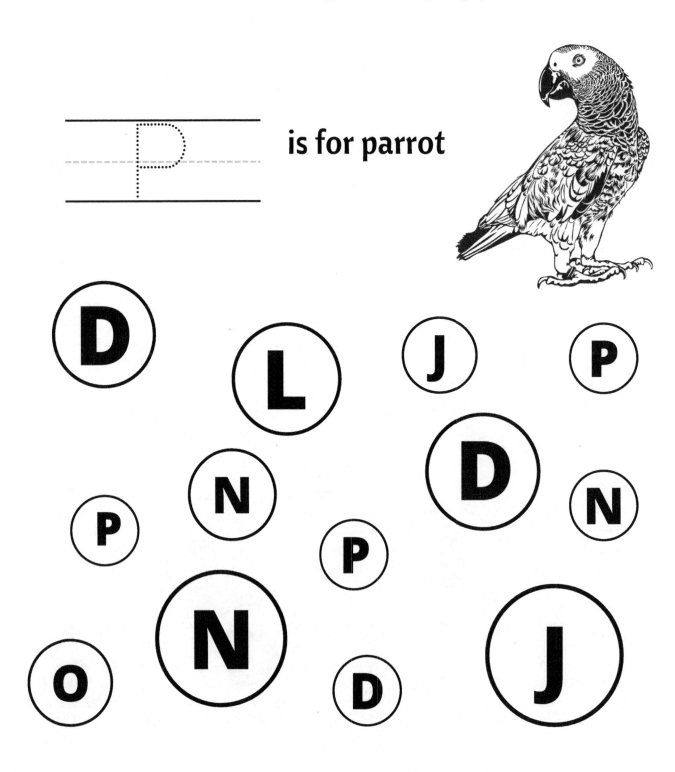

Find the letters.

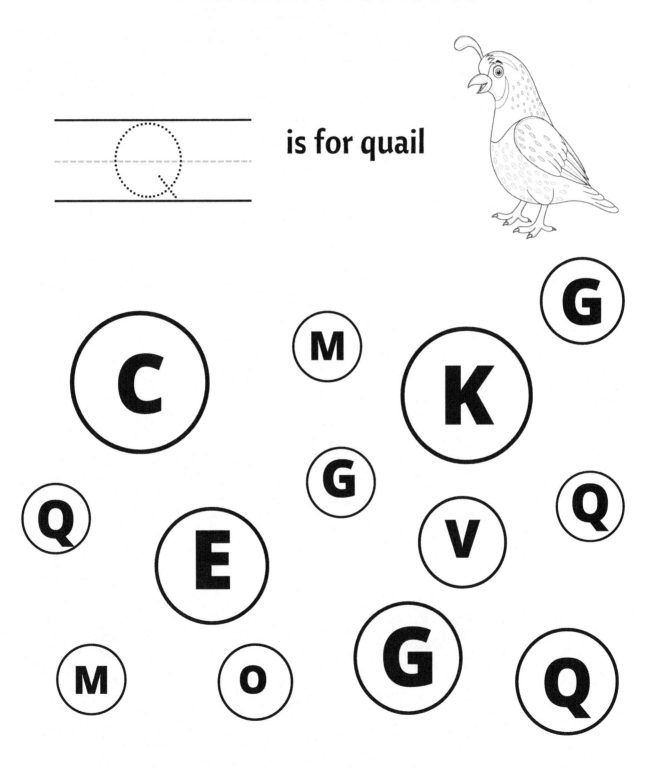

is for quail

Find the letters.

_____R_____ is for rabbit

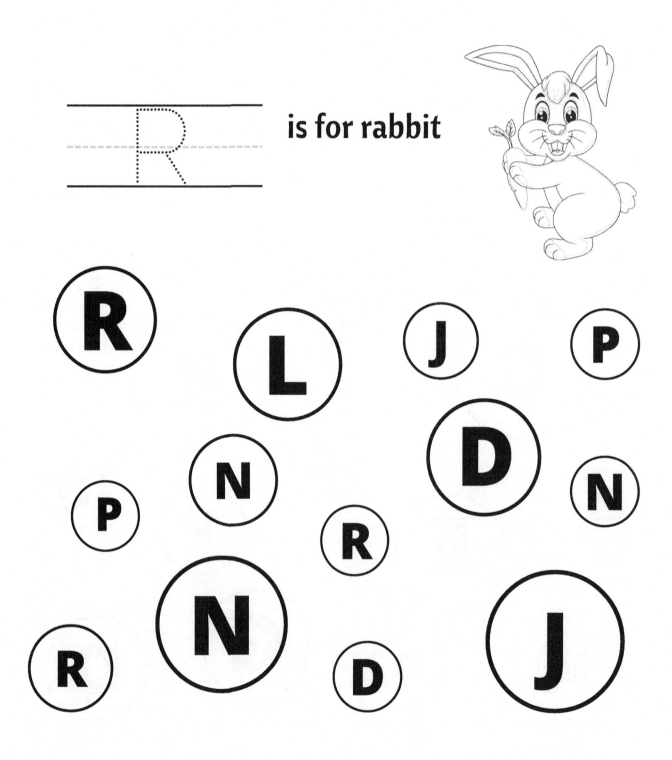

Find the letters.

S   is a snail

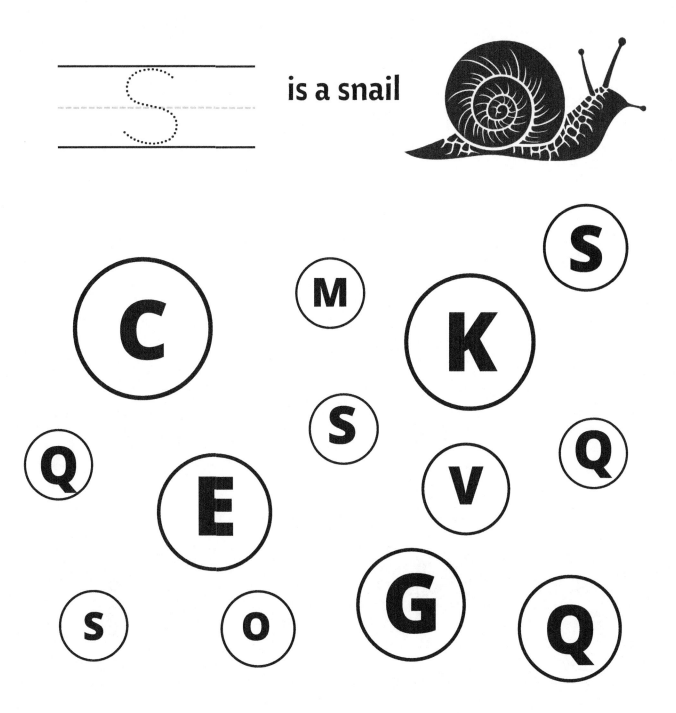

Find the letters.

_____ is for turtle

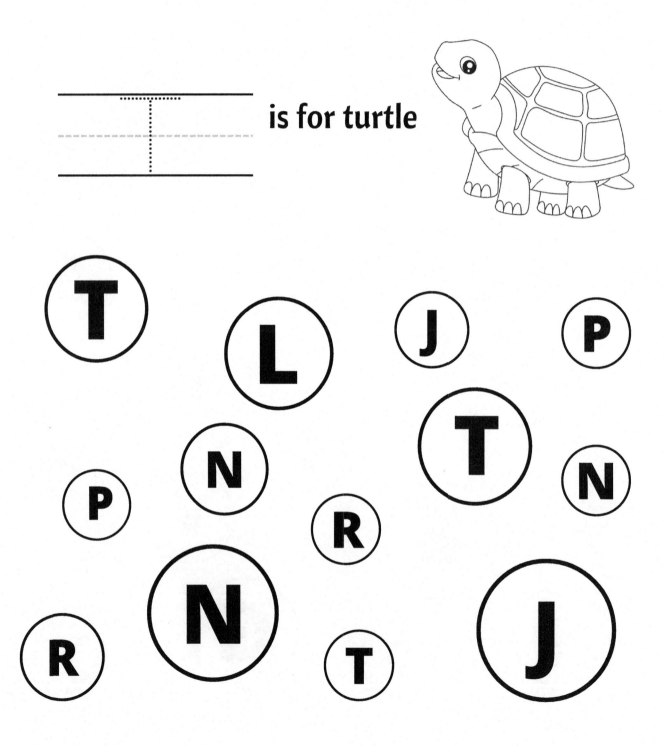

Find the letters.

U is for umbrella

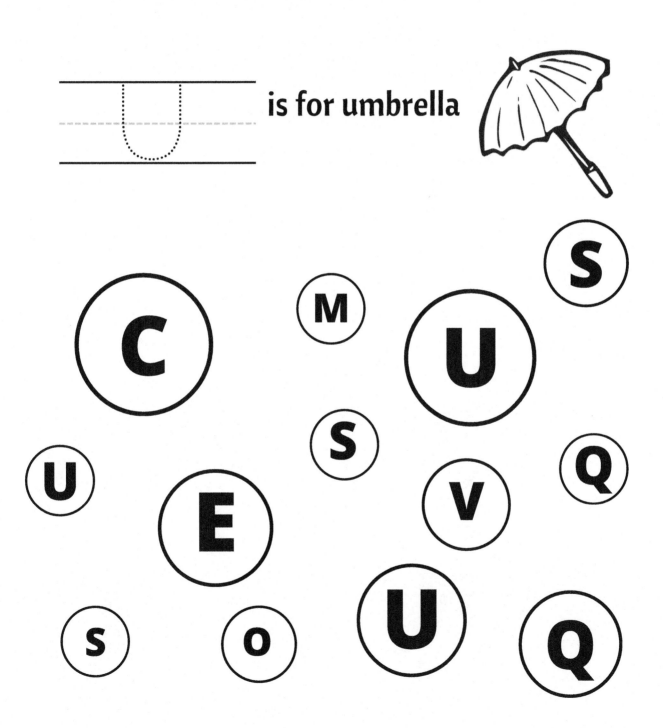

Find the letters.

_____ is for violin

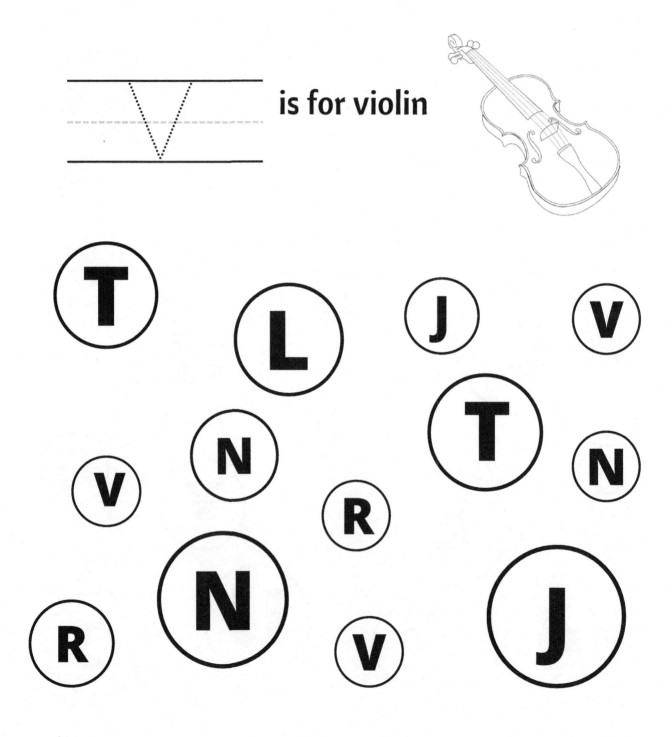

Find the letters.

W   is for whale

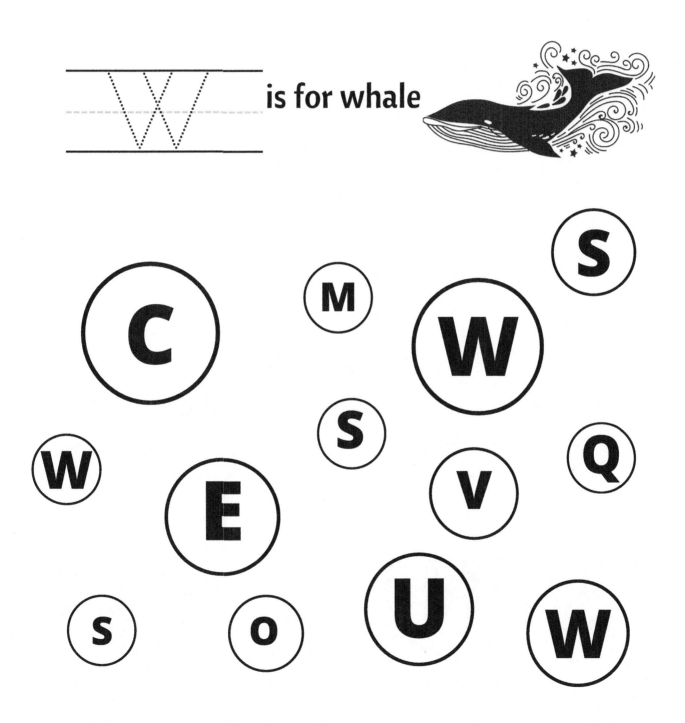

Find the letters.

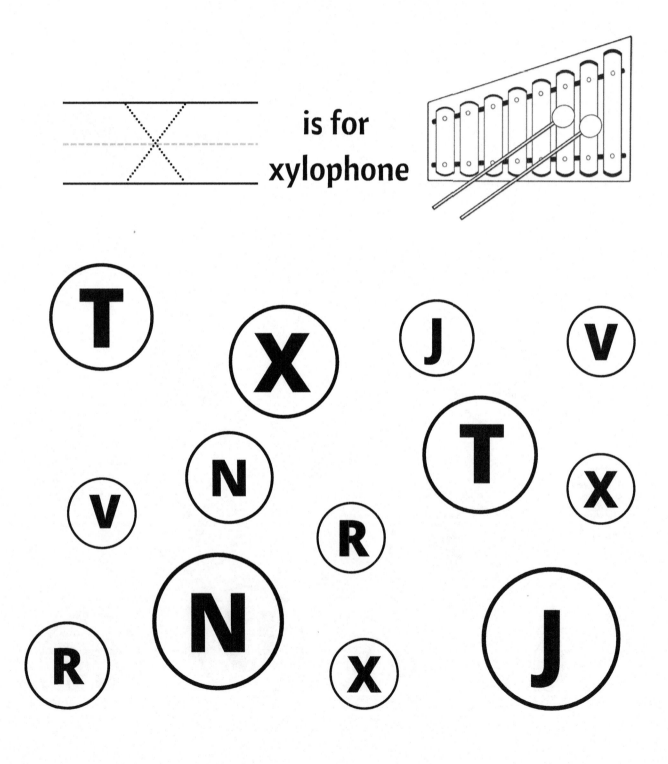

is for
xylophone

Find the letters.

Y is for yak

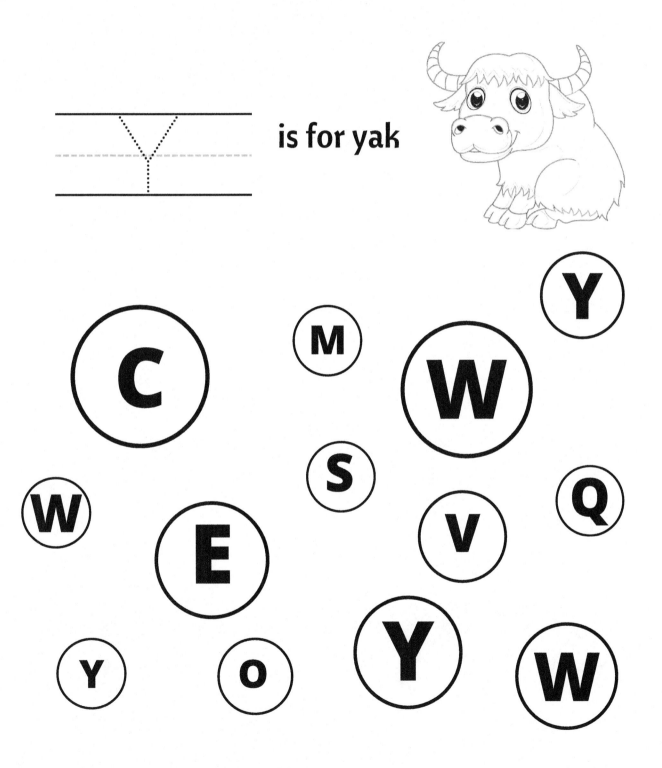

Find the letters.

_____
    Z   is for zebra
_____

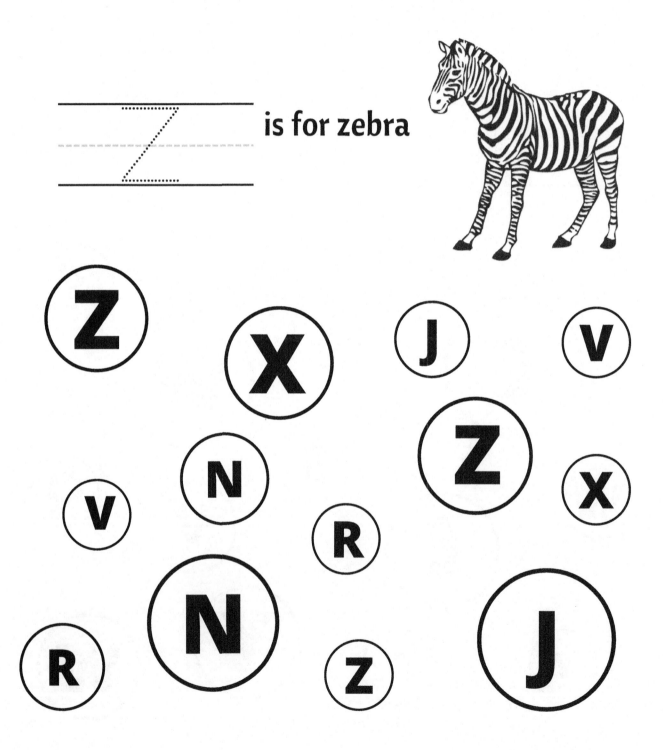

L is for lion and it's also for YOU as you
completed 3 missions

Mission 4:

Count and report!

How many <u>bears</u> are there?

_____

- - - - - - - - - - -

_____

How many <u>roses</u> are there?

_____

_____

_____

How many <u>noodles</u> are there?

_____

_____

How many <u>ice creams</u> are there?

_____

- - - - - - - - - - - - - - -

_____

How many <u>snakes</u> are there?

_____

_____

How many <u>eagles</u> are there?

_____

_ _ _ _ _ _ _ _ _ _ _ _ _

_____

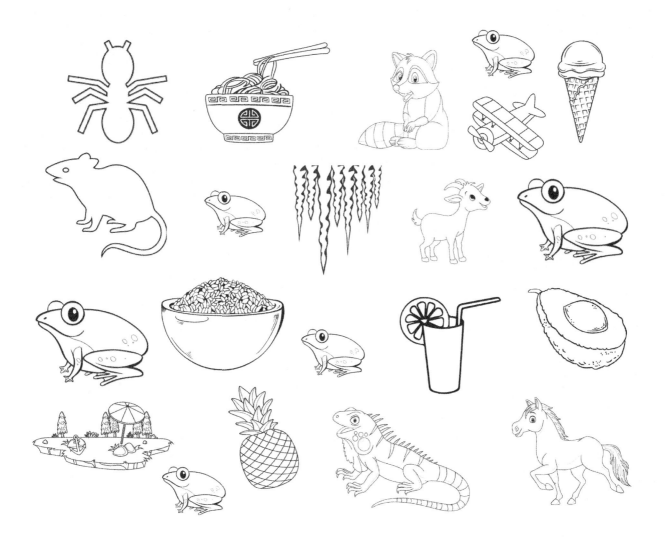

How many <u>frogs</u> are there?

_____

_____

How many <u>earths</u> are there?

_____

- - - - - - - - - - -

_____

How many <u>apples</u> are there?

_____

- - - - - - - - - - - - - - - - - - - -

_____

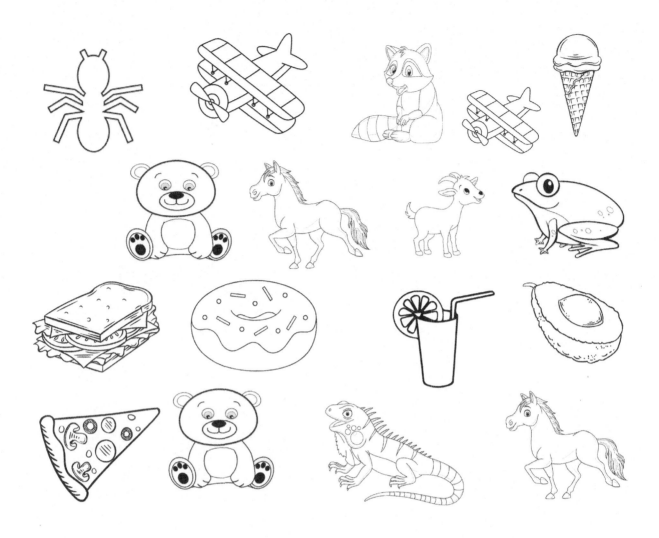

How many <u>horses</u> are there?

_____

_ _ _ _ _ _ _ _ _ _

_____

How many <u>cows</u> are there?

_____

_____

How many <u>ice creams</u> are there?

_____

- - - - - - - - - - - -

_____

How many <u>monkeys</u> are there?

_____

\- \- \- \- \- \- \- \- \- \- \- \- \-

_____

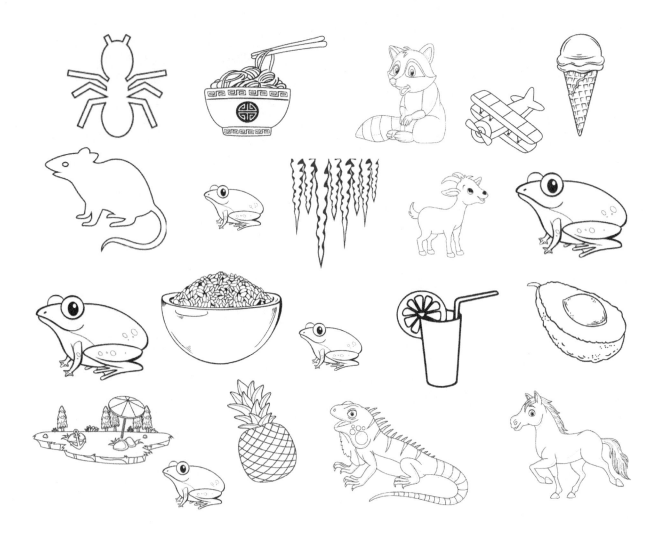

How many <u>earths</u> are there?

_____

- - - - - - - - - -

_____

How many <u>ants</u> are there?

_____

_____

How many <u>avocados</u> are there?

_____

- - - - - - - - - -

_____

How many <u>pizzas</u> are there?

_____

- - - - - - - - - - - -

_____

How many <u>airplanes</u> are there?

_____

_____

_____

How many <u>rice bowls</u> are there?

_____

_____

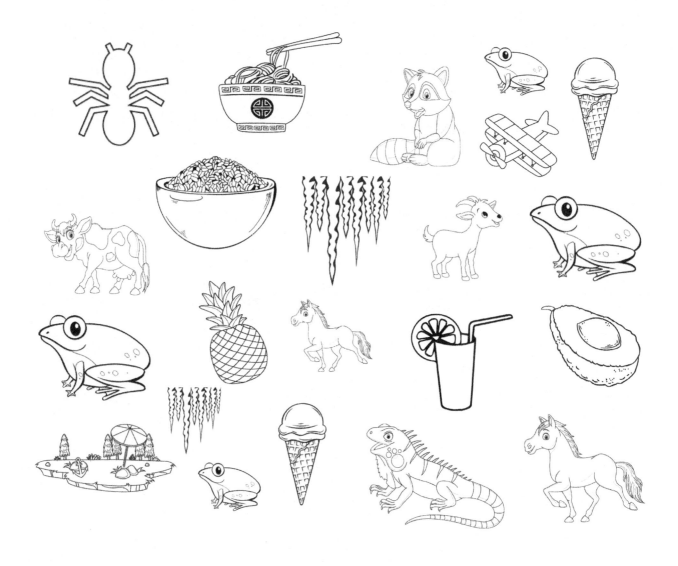

How many <u>icicles</u> are there?

_____

- - - - - - - - - - - - - - - -

_____

How many <u>juices</u> are there?

_____

- - - - - - - - - - - - - -

_____

How many <u>donuts</u> are there?

_____

- - - - - - - - -

_____

How many <u>gloves</u> are there?

_____

_____

How many <u>mice</u> are there?

_____

- - - - - - - - - - - -

_____

How many <u>milks</u> are there?

_____

- - - - - - - - - - - -

_____

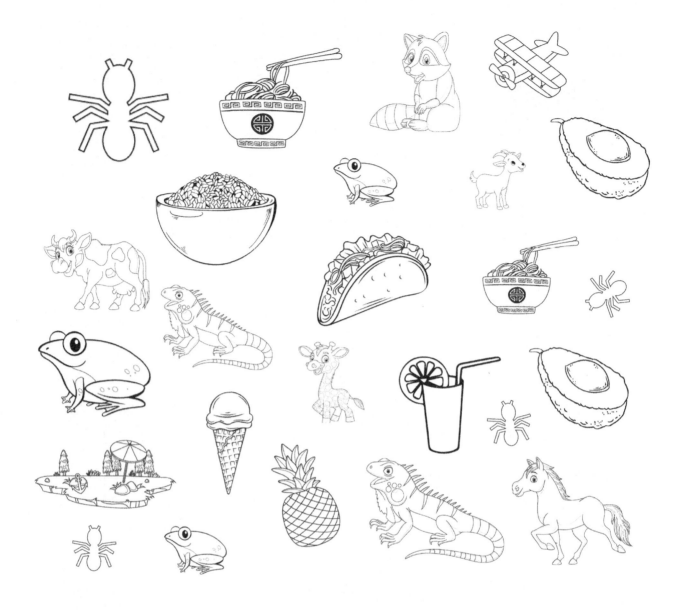

How many <u>iguanas</u> are there?

_____

- - - - - - - - - - -

_____

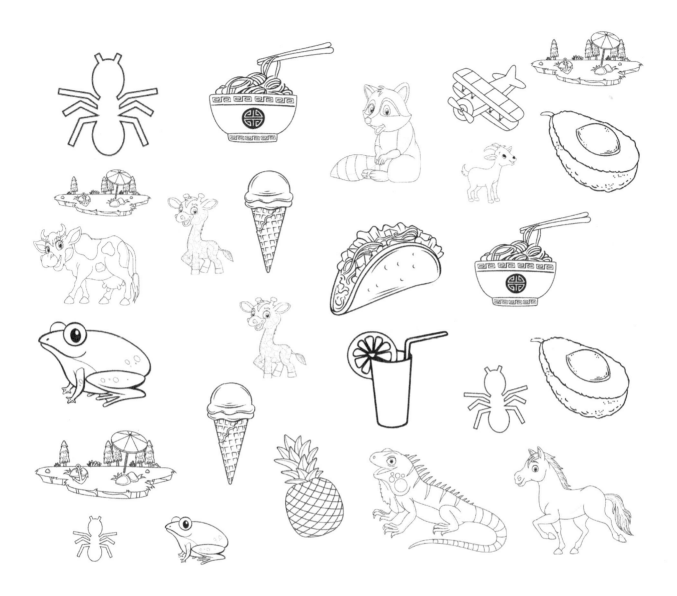

How many <u>islands</u> are there?

_____

_____

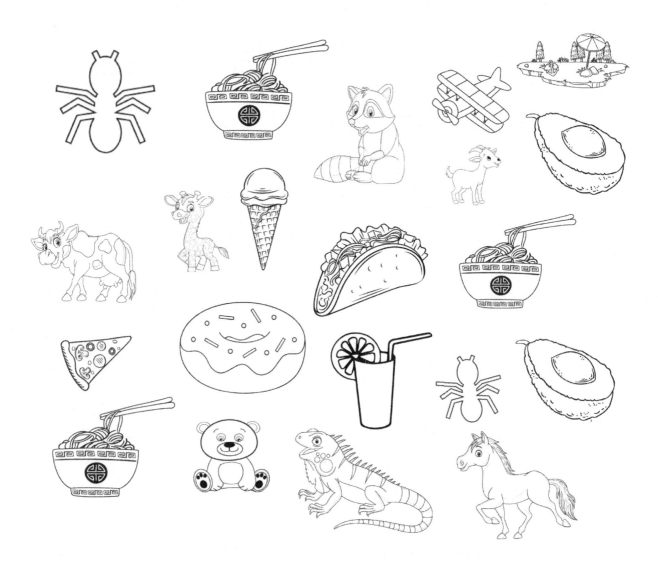

How many __burritos__ are there?

_____

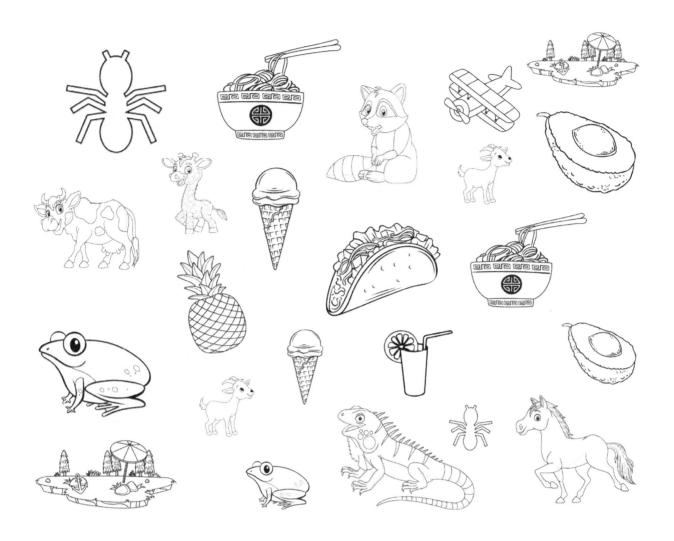

How many <u>goats</u> are there?

_____

- - - - - - - - - - - - - - -

_____

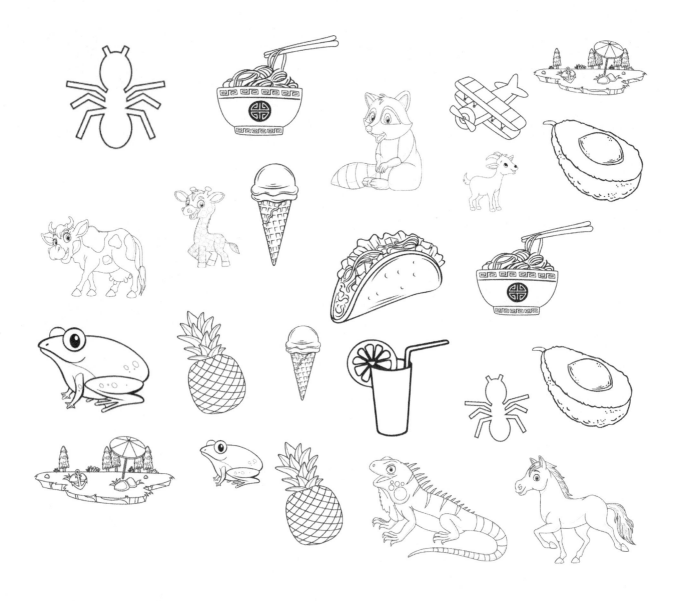

How many <u>donuts</u> are there?

_____

_____

How many <u>gates</u> are there?

_____

- - - - - - - - - - - - -

_____

Congratulations!

You are amazing!

A word from the author

I hope you enjoyed this activity book and it brought you the results you needed. More so, I hope it provided hours of fun, learning, conclusions and excitement.

If that is the case, I would request that you turn your attention briefly back to Amazon, the very place this adventure started! As this is the only place these works are available and as you can provide valuable feedback for others by simply doing a few clicks and writing a few words, I would request you check your e-mail or simply trace your steps back to the book and provide a brief and honest review. And certainly recommend the book to others in your circle!

Kind regards,

T.

Printed in Great Britain
by Amazon

33652443R00084